YOU'RE A
LEADER,
CHARLIE BROWN

Foreword by *New York Times* bestselling motivational author,
Brian Tracy

Published by Simple Truths, an imprint of Sourcebooks, Inc.
P.O. Box 4410, Naperville, Illinois 60567–4410
(630) 961-3900
Fax: (630) 961-2168
www.sourcebooks.com

Printed and bound in the United States of America.

WOZ 10 9 8 7 6 5 4 3 2 1

In honor of Charles Schulz

Photo by Jean Schulz, courtesy of the Charles M. Schulz Museum and Research Center

Contents

Foreword

Your ability to take charge, to lead, to get the best out of yourself and others, is vital to you achieving your full potential in life. A leader is someone who takes action, achieves goals, and moves ahead. What this means is that you can be a leader without followers—the standard of leadership is your ability to get results. Although, as Charlie Brown can attest, having a group like the *Peanuts* to support and follow you always helps.

This definition of leadership is true not just for the *Peanuts* but for all of us. What results do you demand of yourself? Of your team? When you begin to think and act like a leader, you soon get the results that leaders get and enjoy—respect, esteem, more opportunities, and a life of significance. As the *Peanuts* characters will soon show you, that is what creates a real leader. Making a real difference in your world.

Your ability to take charge, to lead, to get the best out of yourself is vital to you achieving your full potential in life—to make the positive changes to our world that all of us are hoping to achieve. Growing up, Charles Schulz's *Peanuts* characters inspired me with their aptitude for kindness and caring. As an adult, I worked to translate that care into my ambitions. How could I grow myself to better aid my community? To better grow my business and provide success at a global scale? This book will provide you with a map to successful leadership—all while keeping the kindness and care from the *Peanuts* at the heart of your actions. We could all better learn how to be loyal like Snoopy, strong like Lucy, and determined like our dear Charlie Brown. I am sure you will enjoy even as you learn and, once you've finished, you yourself will have the tools you need to change the world.

Best,

Brian Tracy

Introduction

Dear Reader,

If you read *Peanuts* every day, you know exactly who Charles Schulz is. Each member of the *Peanuts* gang represents a part of his personality, all of us—including Snoopy, who was inspired by Schulz's childhood dog, Spike.

On any given day, we can be as shy and withdrawn as Charlie Brown, as pushy as Lucy, as introspective as Linus, as raucous as Peppermint Patty, as zealous as Schroeder, as sunny as Sally, or as self-absorbed as Snoopy.

Yet no matter our mood, each and every day, we all strive to be leaders in our fields, to our family, or of our own goals. Reflecting on what *Peanuts* can teach us, we unlock inspiration for each day of our lives.

All of us have gotten to know each character pretty well over the comic strip's fifty-year run. We've appreciated the individual strengths and the challenges each character has faced. No matter their foibles, they each bring something truly unique to their encounters with family and friends—finding success in their own unique journeys.

The concept of leadership was never top of mind when Schulz was writing or drawing the strip, but it's easy to recognize that the *Peanuts* gang displays so many admirable qualities in their day-to-day interactions—Schulz's own inspirational personality shines through. In the pages that follow, we hope that you will find the advice each character shares to be both eloquent and enlightened. And, as comic strip characters, pretty out of the box.

Happy Reading!

Carla Curtsinger

A leader is one who
knows the way,
goes the way, and
shows the way.

John C. Maxwell

Perseverance

"NEVER EVER EVER GIVE UP"
by Charlie Brown

I know what you're thinking: Charlie Brown is giving advice on being a leader? I'm as surprised as you are. I mean, I'm a pretty average kid—below average, most days. And I lose more times than I win.

But I've hit a game-winning home run, and I even

won a game of marbles once, so I know what winning feels like. That next victory could be just around the corner...one more try away.

So I keep trying.

Good grief—I think that could be it!

I may be a loser. Kids even call me a blockhead. But if there's one thing I'm not, it's a quitter. I always show up, and I never lose hope. And here's how I think I do it.

Learn from Failures (I've Had a Few)

You probably know that I'm the leader and pitcher of our baseball team. And we lose most of the time, although we have won a few games (usually when I'm not playing).

But I don't sit around wishing to win—I put in the work! Take my pitching for the team. I know that it really needs to improve. So, last winter, I went out to the ball field every day—when it was still covered in snow— and practiced on my trusty mound.

Ask Snoopy and Woodstock—they were there, along with a bunch of snow baseball fans that they built to cheer me on.

Take a Risk or Two

I've also directed our Christmas pageant—the gang asked me to! True, none of the actors paid much attention to me, and they made fun of the scrawny little tree that I picked out. But it looked fantastic once it was decorated, and we all enjoyed singing carols.

Their faith gave me the drive to see the pageant to its successful end, even when it seemed like nothing would go right.

Have (Gulp) Courage

I have been known to let people—especially girls—get the better of me. Will I ever get up the nerve to talk to the Little Red-Haired Girl? (She's so pretty!) And don't get me started on Lucy and that darn football.

But sometimes courage simply means doing something different from the rest of your friends...like the year I decided to stay home and spend the summer with Snoopy when the rest of the gang went to camp.

You have to listen to that little voice in your head and make the decision that's right for you. It won't always make you popular. But it'll be right, and that's more important.

Get Yourself a Gang

I mentioned that I lose a lot, right? Some people might even say my streak of bad luck is legendary. Maybe you know how that feels.

If you do—and even if you don't—I recommend surrounding yourself with positive people who will pick you up when you're feeling down and help you when you can't accomplish your goals on your own.

I've got Snoopy and Sally, Linus, Lucy, Schroeder, and the whole gang. We might not agree on everything, but when a fastball blows by me on the pitcher's mound, I know they'll pick me up and dust me off.

About That Darn Football

Have I ever been tempted to give up and not kick the ball? Pretty much every time Lucy asks! But she always has a new, convincing reason and so much enthusiasm that I know I have to try again.

Then she pulls always the football at the last minute, and I end up staring up at the sky, yet again, flat on my back. But I keep trying. I keep persevering. And whatever your "football" is, you should too.

HERE'S HOW:

- **Visualize the Goal:** Mine is kicking the football. What's yours? A promotion? A new job? If you're not sure, think about what you really want in life and how this goal will help you today and in the future.
- **Make a List:** What steps will get you to that goal? What resources will you need? Work backwards.
- **Don't Work Alone:** I have my gang; find yours—and whatever other resources you need to make your goal a reality. They are essential to not only achieving your vision but also to helping you celebrate your achievements.
- **Be Positive:** Don't dwell on stumbles or struggles along the way. (I may be a bit guilty of this myself.) Try to expect the best from yourself and the situation at hand. Remain optimistic.
- **Keep Trying:** Every failure takes you one step closer to the day you actually succeed. Every miss takes me one step closer to actually kicking that football.

It will happen—for both of us—one day soon!

How Lucy has convinced me to kick the ball

- Cried
- Rushed me
- Convinced me she was a "changed" person
- Said "Only a muscle spasm will make me move the ball"
- Held it still for a moment
- Used reverse psychology
- Got Rerun to hold the ball for her
- Said the odds were in my favor
- Gave me a signed document (but it wasn't notarized)
- Printed programs for the kick
- Quoted scripture
- Lectured me on trust
- We shook on it
- Sounded sincere
- Said she would be depressed if I didn't

"Good grief,
Charlie Brown,
you got it all wrong!"

PERSEVERANCE: ADDITIONAL POINTS FROM LUCY

Charlie Brown, you're such a blockhead.

I've thoroughly enjoyed this stroll down memory lane. But you're right—you'll never stop trying to kick that football...no matter what I tell you!

BUT TWO IMPORTANT POINTS TO ADD:

- **Violet Started It:** She was the first member of the gang to pull the football out from under you. I simply saw the genius in it!

- **Creativity Is Key:** Okay, so maybe pulling the football out from under you isn't the nicest thing to do (although it is so much fun). But what about all the different ways I talked you into it? Creativity means this proud tradition never gets old.

Anything to add, Violet?

"No comment."

What Have We Learned?

- *Learn from failures.*
- *Get yourself a gang.*
- *Visualize the goal.*
- *Be positive.*

Presence

"I'M A POSITIVE FORCE"
by Lucy

Has Charlie Brown finally stopped talking? Good grief!
He can be a real downer, but don't you worry—Lucy is
on the case! And I've never made a mistake in my life.

(I thought I did once, but I was wrong.) So, if you want to have the presence of a leader, I'm the obvious person to talk to. After all...

I define the "It Factor."

Granted, I was born with It. Only a handful of people in the world are so lucky. And as a therapist and natural giver—Charlie Brown, stop smirking!—I believe it is my professional and personal responsibility to share my God-given talents with those less fortunate.

You're welcome.

Pay attention. I'm only going to say this once. (Although you can read it as many times as you'd like.)

Grab 'Em from the Get-Go

Two kids walk onto the baseball field. Who catches your eye?

The kid who stands tall, head up, facing the other

team and the crowd in the stands? Or the one you don't even notice because he shuffles out, head and shoulders down, with seemingly no energy or direction?

The answer is easy: Me. I'm the first kid. I'll always get noticed first. And you can too. Here's how.

Cool for school

Will you always feel that way? No. Should you always look that way? Absolutely.

That is job one. And you do that by being prepared. If I have a test, I study. If I open the psychiatrist booth, I calm my mind and prepare to count the coins. If I ask Charlie Brown to kick the football, I limber up my arm.

Preparation brings calm to your mind.

To bring calm to your body, take a deep breath before you enter a room, take a test, or start an important meeting. Take a quick look in a mirror. You will never be as good-looking as me, but do your best with what you have.

Look into my eyes

Many people simply don't have the nerve. I always look right into people's eyes. I don't want to appear uncertain or sleepy or uninterested. Are people with presence uninterested? Are leaders sleepy? Am I *ever* uncertain?

Absolutely not.

So whether you're speaking to one person or one hundred, look them in the eye. You'll appear more confident and more expert on your topic, even if you're not. Again, you'll have studied and want to appear as prepared as you are.

Speak up

Loud wins. That shouldn't shock anyone, because I always win, and I'm really loud.

But why does loud win? Because when you are louder, you command the attention of your audience, no matter how large. They can understand every word clearly. And most importantly, when you speak louder, you voice has natural energy and enthusiasm, which is simply more interesting to listen to.

Hands and toes

Whether I'm talking to Charlie Brown at the pitcher's mound, giving advice to patients in the booth, or just chatting at the wall, my body language makes my conversation even more compelling.

My posture is solid. My hand gestures are natural, helping me tell whatever story is fascinating the gang. Together, they support my strong eye contact and voice.

Costume drama

I wear the same thing pretty much every day, much like Apple founder Steve Jobs. (People often confused us.) And like Mr. Jobs, I find that one consistent look is part of my presence. It's expected. It's accepted.

17

However, you can also make the argument—and I do like to argue—that choosing your outfit with your audience in mind is an extremely valuable strategy. Why does our baseball team wear the same uniform? To show common goals (and easily identify the losing team). Dressing with your audience in mind is a visual expression of your shared views.

I know it all looks amazing on me, and you might feel a little intimidated. That's perfectly natural.

All I ask is that you try.

"A report by me, Sally..."

PRESENCE: ADDITIONAL POINTS FROM SALLY

This is my show-and-tell on presents.

Let me begin by saying I would never disagree with Lucy. She is smart and pretty and probably listening right now.

But I do believe that your presents should contain a few more things that she just probably forgot to mention. Gifts should contain all the joyful things we all love! After all the best types of presents are... what's that? Oh, we are talking about *presence*? I'm so embarrassed—what will I do with all this extra ribbon! Oh well, I can also talk about presence with presents!

Be friendly

Sometimes when I get up to do a report in front of class, I get nervous. I'm stiff and awkward and can even seem angry when I'm certainly not. I act like a completely different person.

People with presence look natural and warm...like someone you'd want to be friends with every day! And the audience remembers how you make them feel as much as, if not more than, the words that you say.

Be in the room

It's easy to get busy and have your mind go in a hundred different directions. Right now, for example, I'm thinking about what I want for lunch, the test next period I haven't studied for, and my favorite beanbag chair. People with real presents focus on the topic of their report and the people that they're speaking to.

Really speak to people

And speaking of speaking to people...the words you choose are really important. We've all been in class when the lesson goes over our heads...the words are too big, the theories too complicated. A person who has presence knows the people he is talking to and uses words and examples that they understand and respond to. The teachers who do that are my favorite teachers in school.

What Have We Learned?

- *The "It Factor" can be learned.*
- *Your physical habits define your presence.*
- *People remember how you make them feel too.*

Communication

"IT WAS A DARK AND STORMY NIGHT"
by Snoopy

Hello. It is I, the World-Famous Author, writing my next bestseller.

I've actually been writing it for years. While my mind reels with sarcastic comebacks to my critics, second sentences are much harder to come by.

And the blank page is the ugliest thing in the world (next to an empty dog dish).

Fortunately, I am mature enough to listen to my critics when they offer feedback on my writing. I have learned some helpful tips that are useful for anyone wielding a pen, typewriter, computer, or skywriting plane.

Because some people make money from their writing. Now, *that's* a novel idea.

Write What You Know
You should write one of those "how-to" books

I have made many of the same mistakes over and over again (and, some would say, written the same thing over and over again. Where do they get this stuff?).

LEARN FROM MY MISTAKES:

1. **It's Not about You.** Visualize your reader (or readers, if you're luckier than me). Who are they? What is important to them? What interests them most? The more you know about your audience, the more relevant your writing will be.

2. **Speak.** Write as though you are having a conversation with one person. Avoid formal words and phrases that can create a wall between you and your reader. To double-check the flow, read your writing aloud. Your ear will hear awkward words and phrases that your eye might not be able to see. But if you read aloud on top of your doghouse, don't be surprised if you get some funny looks from passersby. And birds. Everyone, actually.

3. **Keep It Simple.** While flowery verse may sell greeting cards, and twenty-page term papers will get you an A in high school, the business world expects less of you—as in clear, concise writing, with the most important point front and center. Short words. Short sentences. Short paragraphs. (I would say more, but on this point will settle for less.)

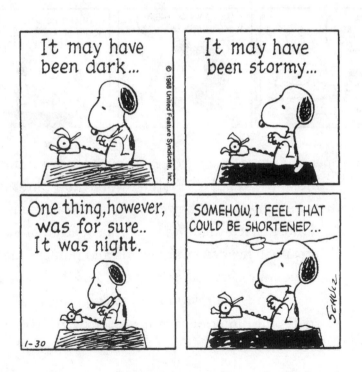

4. **No Inside Jobs.** Avoid using words, phrases, or acronyms that are specific to your company or technical and academic, because they might confuse or even annoy your reader. For example, I only use the term "author" when I think there are people around who might buy one of my books.

5. **Pick Your Verbs.** When I re-read my latest bestseller, I always scan for "be" verbs—*am, is, are, was, were.* Using them too frequently indicates weak verb choices. See if you can substitute another stronger, more action-oriented verb instead. Your writing will sing!

6. **It's All about the Treats.** Don't just describe the features of your product or idea; instead, make benefit statements that connect with the reader. For example, water is calorie-free (feature), and water refreshes and hydrates you (benefit). That reminds me—where is my water bowl?

7. **Looks Matter.** The way your writing looks is just as important as the words themselves. (That's why I write my novels in that cool Gothic script.) In fact, readers decide in the first three seconds whether or not they are going to read a document at all, and it's based on looks. Use formatting tools (bold, bullets,

underline) to make your writing look more attractive to your audience.

8. **End Strong.** Include a clear call to action for your reader at the end so they know what must be done, and make it as easy as possible. You should practically do it for them.

Yesterday, I was a dog. Today, I'm a dog. Tomorrow, I'll probably still be a dog. But if I follow my own advice, I'll be a dog with a published novel and a book tour.

"Your first draft always needs a lot of work, Snoopy, and these writing tips are no exception."

COMMUNICATION: ADDITIONAL POINTS FROM LUCY

Might I suggest the following additions? (I'm not really asking. Here they are.)

Proofreading

DOS

× **Leave Some Time**—a day, if possible—between writing and proofreading. The time and distance allow you to be more objective and to see more room for improvement.

× **Proofread from the Outside In**. Start with paragraph structure. Then, look at individual sentences. Next, review your word choice. Finally, check spelling and punctuation.

× **A Second Pair of Eyes Is Always Best.** Ask a friend to proofread your document for you. (And no, Snoopy, not Woodstock.)

DON'TS

× **Proofread on the Computer Screen.** Work from printed copies.

✗ Depend on Spell-check. It can check spelling, but not context or word choice.

✗ Keep Writing "It Was a Dark and Stormy Night." Good grief!

"Snoopy, I think you
did a great job on the
writing tips!"

COMMUNICATION: ADDITIONAL POINTS FROM CHARLIE BROWN

Your years of novel writing shine through your thoughtful recommendations.

But, as leader of the baseball team, I've had some experience with business communications that, sadly, a dog could not. So maybe we should discuss a couple of things to keep in mind when you're writing for a corporate audience.

- **Do Your Research:** Do you know the assistant or support staff? They can give you valuable tips into their preferred style of communication.
- **Be Concise:** Your audience won't necessarily share your interest in the topic, or have time to read extensive notes. A one- to two-page executive summary is always a safe bet.
- **Make It Easy:** Remember to use formatting tools that make your communication easy to skim.
- **Think in Terms of Fixes:** Don't simply identify problems; bring solutions to the table.

Listening

"BUTTERNUT BREAD KEEPS YOUR EARS WARM"
by Linus

I take it by the look on your face that you've never used butternut bread as earmuffs.

It's very effective and earth-friendly...you can eat the slices after the chill has passed. (Just go light on the butter, or you'll have a hard time hearing.)

I've been wearing mine in the pumpkin patch. Each

What Have We Learned?

- *Write for your audience in a concise yet conversational style.*
- *Use formatting elements to make your document easy to skim.*
- *Allow ample time for proofreading—have a friend proofread if possible.*

4

Listening

"BUTTERNUT BREAD KEEPS YOUR EARS WARM"
by Linus

I take it by the look on your face that you've never used butternut bread as earmuffs.

It's very effective and earth-friendly...you can eat the slices after the chill has passed. (Just go light on the butter, or you'll have a hard time hearing.)

I've been wearing mine in the pumpkin patch. Each

year, the Great Pumpkin rises out of the patch that he thinks is the most sincere.

I was sure he would pick mine. You can look around and see that there's not a sign of hypocrisy! Nothing but sincerity as far as the eye can see.

What was that?

(pause)

What was that?

Did you hear anything? I thought that was the Great Pumpkin. Of course, you really have to listen to hear him. And people aren't very good at listening...even when we try really hard.

It's not our fault. **It's all part of the evolutionary process.**

It's Not Life-or-Death, Charlie Brown

As the threat of our natural predators has decreased throughout time, and through advancements in technology, our sense of hearing has dulled. With the exception of loud noises that we associate with danger—like sirens and alarms—we filter out most sounds.

Even when we pay close attention to someone, it can be difficult to recall details of a conversation.

Now, most of my discussions aren't life-or-death, although Charlie Brown sometimes thinks they are. (I'm sure you've heard him talk about the Little Red-Haired Girl. Will he ever get up the nerve to talk to her?) But if we take time to practice the way we listen, we can improve this very important skill.

Good listeners build stronger relationships, resolve conflicts, and make fewer mistakes. So, let's talk about how we can all be better listeners.

Do You Have Any Teammates Who Listen?

Charlie Brown is my best friend. We spend a lot of time together. On any given day, you might see us on the ball field, sitting on a curb, or leaning up against our favorite brick wall, talking about school, baseball, or life in general.

I've learned a lot about what it takes to be a good listener in my conversations with Charlie Brown.

Pay Attention (and Show It)

Put away your papers, your phone, and your computer, and focus on the other person. (I even put down my blanket—the ultimate sacrifice—to listen to Charlie Brown.)

Look into their eyes. It shows respect and forms a real connection. Don't stare; look away from time to time. And use positive body language—an enthusiastic tone of voice, uncrossed arms, and a slight lean forward—to show you are present.

Ask Focused Questions

A good listener needs to ask the right kind of questions to get the information they need.

Think like Joe Reporter and ask open-ended questions that will help you understand: who, what, when, why, where, how. Make sure they are focused on the topic at hand; don't use a question as an opportunity to change the subject or move the focus onto yourself.

To clarify information, ask questions that encourage greater detail. Some examples include:

- Could you please repeat...?
- Can you tell me more about...?
- How would you describe...?
- When you said _____, what exactly did you mean?
- Would you explain how...?

Note What Isn't Being Said Too

Good listeners know how to put themselves in the other person's shoes and feel what they are feeling at that moment. They use empathy.

People's words alone don't tell the entire story. The look in their eyes, the tension in their mouth, the set

of their shoulders—these can reveal much more. How many times has Charlie Brown told me he was "fine" when it was clear that something was amiss? (Of course, most of the time we had just lost a baseball game, so I had a pretty good idea that he was upset.)

Don't Judge

When I play second base for the ball team, I spend a lot of time standing at the pitcher's mound, talking to Charlie Brown. He's the leader of the team, but he's always willing to listen to suggestions from me or other members of the gang. Charlie Brown may be a bit of a blockhead, but he's open-minded. He listens and learns and tries to change. But do we win? No, no, we never really do.

I can't stand it.

Remain Silent

I have been teased from time to time about my blanket and my thumb-sucking habit. It turns out the two have helped me with one essential part of being a good listener—being quiet.

If you're not asking a question to clarify or ensure

understanding, you shouldn't be talking. Too often, we take over the conversation in our rush to solve the problem before we truly know what it is. Or we inadvertently turn attention to ourselves or our own problems.

I recommend the 80/20 rule in any conversation: My partner should be speaking 80 percent of the time; I should be speaking 20 percent. That is the goal. Instead of talking, I focus on the words being spoken and create pictures in my mind to aid in my understanding and retention of the information.

Sum It Up

As the conversation concludes, repeat what you've heard to make sure you both understand. You can then discuss alternate solutions, if any, and give feedback.

Listen to This

- Eighty-five percent of what we know, we have learned through listening.
- In a typical business day, we spend
    - ✗ 45 percent of our time listening
    - ✗ 30 percent of our time talking
    - ✗ 16 percent of our time reading
    - ✗ 9 percent of our time writing
- People listen at a 25 percent comprehension rate.

"A cheer for my sweet Babboo! By me, Sally"

LISTENING: ADDITIONAL POINTS FROM SALLY

Two bits,
Four bits,
My Sweet Babboo...
I will always listen to you!

How do I do it?
Here's a clue:
This little rhyme
Named after you.

L I N U S
***L**—LISTEN carefully. Focus on the*
person speaking.
***I**—Provide needed INFORMATION.*
Some details may be missing.
***N**—Put it in a NUTSHELL. Summa-*
rize frequently.
***U**—Try to UNDERSTAND. Consider*
from the other's point of view.
***S**—Discuss SUBSTITUTES. Are*
there alternate solutions?

This process is called active listening, by the way. Of course, a cheerleader like me practices this technique every day, and you should too. Active listening gives you the information you need and helps you make better decisions, which in turn makes you a better leader.

Linus says it also helps you to not talk too much. I have decided not to take that personally.

What Have We Learned?

- *Evolution has made it difficult for us to listen.*
- *Pay attention when you listen (and show it).*
- *Use the LINUS mnemonic to become an active listener.*

The most
important thing
in communication
is hearing what
isn't said.

Peter Drucker

5

Inspiration

"THE JOY IS IN THE PLAYING"
by Schroeder

I am usually quite content to play my piano and let other members of the gang speak. About anything. In any situation.

But on the topic of inspiration, I must push back the piano bench, stand up, and take center stage. Because everything I am, everything I have accomplished, and everything I hope to become I owe to one man, and one man only...

The incomparable Beethoven, the greatest of all composers. The wonderful pianist and tower of strength.

Beethoven wrote nine symphonies, sixteen string quartets, thirty-two piano sonatas, the opera *Fidelio*, five piano concertos, a violin concerto, two masses, and numerous chamber music compositions, songs, choral works, and orchestra overtures...and over half of these he composed after losing his hearing.

His unparalleled talent and ability have motivated me to play complicated pieces on my toy piano...and my black keys are only painted on.

(I practice **a lot**.)

While his revolutionary compositions are amazing on their own merit—they break all the rules, elicit every emotion—Beethoven the man inspires even more.

He Is the Greatest

Beethoven did not fit the stereotypical image of a leader. He didn't wear a business suit or have carefully styled hair...quite the opposite. But leaders today are breaking that old cookie-cutter mold, and I think people will be inspired—as I am—by the qualities that define his well-known genius.

Overcoming obstacles

Beethoven showed great aptitude and enthusiasm for music at a very young age, and his father ensured that he received lessons in piano and violin. He even studied under Mozart. But when his mother became ill, Beethoven returned home, and after her death, he took care of his two siblings at her request. Yet he still managed to make music and a name for himself. And when his hearing began to fail at the age of thirty, he continued to compose. In fact, half of Beethoven's nine symphonies were written after he was completely deaf.

Great leaders find their passion and pursue it at any cost. Me? I manage to practice with Lucy hanging around. Now, *that's* an obstacle.

Being true to yourself

Beethoven had no patience for court and all its rules of etiquette, and he was not shy about saying so. If he was performing and the audience was being inattentive, he would simply stop. Lucky for him, Archduke Rudolph decreed that Beethoven did not have to follow the rules of court.

I feel a real kinship with the maestro here. I don't do things like the rest of the gang, and they support my choices. I can simply be me. And therein lies the lesson: Develop a personal leadership style (emphasis on "personal"). Don't try to fit in; instead, make the situation fit your own unique personality.

Earning people's trust

As eccentric as Beethoven was, he was surrounded by loyal friends, including his assistant Ferdinand Ries. His friends even competed with each other to take care of him in his later years. How did he inspire such trust? The same way you and I can:

- **Show an Interest in Others:** Let them know that you care about their lives, both their career successes and their relationships with their family and friends.
- **Have a Sense of Humor:** (Beethoven was notorious for pranks and practical jokes.)

- **Calmly Manage and Correct Mistakes,** instead of berating people in anger. (Beethoven did not always follow this last tip.)

Remaining innovative

Good leaders are always looking for new ideas and new information. They have natural curiosity and are always learning. While Beethoven already inspired with a musical genius that transcended deafness, his quest to beat his hearing loss was mind-boggling. A variety of ear trumpets littered his rooms, and he played a piano especially built for him with extra strings and a resonator.

Amazing. And I'm still waiting for real black keys on my piano.

Building a legacy

No one, not even Lucy, will dispute the fact that the incomparable Beethoven, the greatest of all composers, has a legacy. His groundbreaking music, the movies devoted to his work, and the gold record of his music that is flying around the galaxy on the *Voyager* spacecraft are proof enough.

The real lesson is that Beethoven achieved this legacy without compromising his principles. He knew the type of work he wanted to leave behind, but refused to abandon his commitment to the Enlightenment, even when it wasn't popular.

We must all know what is nonnegotiable as we strive to build our legacy. (Lucy—for me, that means remaining single like the maestro.)

These are some of the reasons I've celebrated Beethoven's birthday twenty-seven times throughout the years. (It's December 16, by the way.) He is a daily source of inspiration.

"So Schroeder is inspired by Beethoven?"

INSPIRATION: ADDITIONAL POINTS FROM LUCY

We all saw that coming a mile away—am I right?

It's a classic case of hero worship. I've seen it before in the psychiatry biz. It won't do him any harm, of course, but...

What about the other heroes that Schroeder knows? That he sees every day? Don't they inspire him?

There's a saying: "You are the average of the five people you spend the most time with."

Perhaps Schroeder can find inspiration in the things these people do for him...especially if one of them is me. I certainly bring up the average.

Consider Beethoven for a moment. Who were his five people? Perhaps his mother Maria Magdalena van Beethoven. Or Antonie Brentano, who allegedly inspired "Immortal Beloved." Or Therese Malfatti, whom Beethoven wanted to marry. Any of these great women could have inspired Beethoven by

- caring for him;
- challenging him;
- redirecting his path;

- speaking the truth; and/or
- listening to him.

I do the same things for Schroeder! I should be an inspiration to his music and his life.

I can't stand it.

What Have We Learned?

- *Great leaders find their passions and pursue them at any cost.*
- *Great leaders are always looking for new ideas and new information.*
- *You are the average of the five people you spend the most time with.*

The best and most
beautiful things in the
world cannot be seen
or even touched—
they must be felt
with the heart.

Helen Keller

Teamwork

"WE CAN DO IT"
by Peppermint Patty

Hey. You a friend of Chuck?

Because any friend of Chuck is a friend of mine. That kid with the big nose too—Snoopy. They're the best.

That surprises some people—how Chuck and I can be such good friends even though my baseball team beats his, every single game. (Crushes them, actually.)

Heck, there are no bad feelings between Chuck and me. We know how to lead our teams out of victory and defeat, and come out on the other side feeling optimistic regardless of the outcome.

Wait—that's just me.

Chuck is a great loser. I even let him join my team once. He sold popcorn and was our team mascot for a while. But he kept wanting to actually play baseball...so I had to let him go.

I've had to make a lot of difficult decisions as team captain. But every decision was for the good of my players...to make the team want to be better. Do better. And give their very best every day in support of each other.

Whoa. That took a lot of energy. I need a nap.

Keep Your Eye on the Ball (and Get a Bigger Glove)

When you've led a team to as many victories as I have,

you figure out the keys to creating and maintaining a motivated, focused squad.

1. Own your personal style

A lot of leaders have Type A personalities—driven, focused, always at the head of the class. Me?

Not so much.

In fact, one of my teachers inducted me into the "D-Minus Hall of Fame." I would have missed the ceremony too, if Marcie hadn't woken me up.

So, you could say my leadership style is a little laid-back. Allows for more naps. Includes team practices that start a bit late because I slept through my alarm. Again.

Now, I'm not saying that this is the best or only way to lead a team. Absolutely not! You just need to be aware of your personal leadership style, and ask yourself:

- Is my style effective with this particular team?
- Have they accepted me as their leader?
- Are there changes I can make that will benefit the team or our project?

Remember, you're ultimately responsible for the team's success or failure, so you need to step up and do what's right, even if your team doesn't appreciate your effort. Leaders aren't always popular like me.

2. Identify individual strengths...

Every member of a team is different, and that makes a leader's job easy. But every member of a team is different, and that makes a leader's job difficult.

See what I did there?

(My teacher says I talk in circles a lot. But in this case, it's the truth.)

As the team leader, you have to spend some time evaluating the strengths and weaknesses that each team member brings to the table. Then you have to figure out the best way to use those strengths to meet your goals, and minimize the weaknesses so they don't get in the way of your project's ultimate success.

So where do you start?

- Make a list.
- Have the team members make one too.
- Ask other team members for input.

- Consult past feedback from your teammates.
- Compare all the lists and prioritize.

That's why my weakest player is always in right field, where they can do less damage—sorry, Marcie—and why Charlie Brown didn't actually play baseball at all when he was on the team way back when.

If you don't take the time to get to know the people who are working with you, victory will always be out of reach.

3. ...and help them work as a team

Once you know your team members really well, make sure they each (1) know their role and (2) understand exactly what is expected of them in that role.

Easy, right? It's not.

For one thing, your team members won't always want the role they are assigned. So while you are busy explaining why the role is important to the team and what tasks need to be completed, they are still stewing over the fact that they aren't pitching in the big game!

I mean...doing the role they really want to do.

Your success as a leader depends not only on your ability to put the right people into the right positions, but also on your success in communicating that news in such a way that everyone understands and accepts their positions within the grand scheme of things. Because it's hard to comprehend that you aren't the star player you think you are. Maybe you belong on the B Team, which is still an important role to the overall success of the team.

4. Give lots of pointers

If you want your team to stay on track, you have to talk

constantly. (Ask my teachers. I'm in detention all the time for my unwelcome opinions.)

Tell your team what's working and what's not every day. If you wait to give feedback until you have a really big problem, it will be even harder to recover and move forward.

Like that time I unwisely decided to leave school and live in Chuck's guesthouse. Because of a lack of communication, I didn't realize I was living in Snoopy's doghouse.

Let's just say my pride had the flu on that one. And it all could have been prevented.

Make feedback part of your team's daily routine, both formal and informal. Give pointers

- at team and individual meetings;
- in emails;
- during quick phone calls;
- in texts and IMs; and/or
- during public announcements.

Also, realize that what works for one team might not work for another. Just as every individual on your team is unique, the type of feedback and communication that proves effective will be different as well.

5. Pass out candy... I mean compliments

We all have a favorite thing. Mine is sleep.

Know what your team likes, and when you're passing out really big compliments, occasionally add a gift of their favorite thing. Too many leaders take their best team members for granted, and don't realize how much that little extra bit of recognition can mean.

It's like when I'm practicing my ice skating with Snoopy—he's my coach, in case you didn't know—and he praises me and kisses me on the nose...

I can do a triple axel (or, at least, I feel like I can).

Recognizing and respecting your team's hard work are essential to building loyalty and trust (and may inspire them to put in a little extra effort next time around).

"One more thing about teamwork!"

TEAMWORK: ADDITIONAL POINTS FROM FRANKLIN

One thing I think I am uniquely able to speak on is the importance of teamwork and sportsmanship even outside of your own team! Whenever I visit from our neighborhood, I always feel welcomed by the kids here in Charlie Brown's neighborhood. Particularly on your team, Patty, I have always felt welcomed by true friends. You have a gift in bringing people together! You in particular have helped me practice and play hockey even though you don't understand my dreams of going pro. Even though you don't share my dream, you have helped me work toward achieving it for myself! Building people up and helping them grow is a part of who you and the gang are. I am thankful for the support, as are all the other kids in the neighborhood!

What Have We Learned?

- *Know what kind of leader you are.*
- *Acknowledge your team's unique qualities and bring them together into a stronger unit.*
- *Use feedback to teach and praise.*
- *Make teamwork part of who you are: when your friend achieves, you achieve.*

Loyalty

"MY FAITHFUL DOG WILL RESCUE ME"
by Charlie Brown

Hi. It's me again. I'm hope you've been having a good time with the rest of the gang.

But when I heard this chapter was about loyalty, I had

to jump back in, because I have such a wonderful, loyal friend in Snoopy.

Sure, he likes to pretend he doesn't know my name sometimes, and he calls me "that round-headed kid," but I know he will be right by my side whenever I really need him.

Remember when that bully took my autographed baseball and challenged me to a fight? Snoopy helped me get it back. And when Peppermint Patty insulted me while we were playing Ha Ha Herman, guess who walked out of the game with me?

Snoopy always has my back.

What does true loyalty look like in your life? Team members who display any of these qualities are true loyalists (or dogs like Snoopy).

They Treat You Like a Person

You work together. Some of you work for one another. Loyal team members help each other reach their professional goals, and want what's best for each other in their personal lives as well.

Because you're more than just coworkers or teammates—you're people too.

It's a lot like the Christmas pageant I directed. I needed the gang to work for me on the play. But we were all still friends, and that mattered most of all...which I had to keep reminding myself when they wanted to goof off instead of rehearse!

But because they were loyal to me and to each other, they pulled together and turned in an amazing performance. I can still hear them singing "O Holy Night"... can't you?

They Tell You the Truth

Loyal friends aren't yes-men—or yes-women—regardless of how high up they've climbed the ladder of success. Instead, they tell you what you need to hear, which can sometimes be the last thing you want to hear—that you are wrong or confused or need to stop talking.

Loyal friends step up and tell you the truth because, in the long run, it's the best thing for you or for the team, if you have one. And after the dust has settled, you walk away—still friends.

Case in point: the Little Red-Haired Girl. Snoopy and Linus have kept me honest for years now.

Of course, I am going to talk to her one day soon. (If

they were here right now, they'd both be shaking their heads no. But I still believe.)

They Don't Criticize You in Public...

When you are leading a project—or just in charge for the day—does your team disrespect you and your decisions? Do they mock you in front of everybody? Do they gossip about you and talk behind your back?

That's not loyalty.

Loyal friends and team members support you and set an example on how you should be treated—even when you aren't around to hear.

Like when Sally was being bullied on the playground. Snoopy barked really loudly at anyone who threatened her, and he let her "use" him as her protector. He also helped her write her report on animal friends.

She got an A. (I think it was her first and only one.)

...But They Might Disagree with You in Private

That doesn't mean they aren't honest with you when no one's looking. (Refer to "They Tell You the Truth.") That's one of the best parts of working in teams— different points of view, different opinions, different backgrounds. That diversity makes you stronger and smarter and, honestly, makes work more fun.

But you should only differ in opinion when you are alone together. Present a unified voice to the world.

They're Honest When It's Time to Go

Good-byes are the worst...especially to a friend or teammate who is simply the best. But if they respect and trust you enough to let you know ahead of time that they plan to leave, you need to show them the same degree of loyalty.

They probably know you'll have to work hard to fill the hole they are leaving in your team; that's why they told you.

Heck, when Snoopy left to give a speech at the Daisy Hill Puppy Farm, he was only gone a few days, and it seemed like years. Peppermint Patty wanted to rent out his doghouse while he was gone, but it just wouldn't have been the same.

I was so glad when he came back. Snoopy, never leave again.

"Thanks for letting us know what loyalty looks like, Charlie Brown."

LOYALTY: ADDITIONAL POINTS FROM LUCY

But real leaders are doers like me. We build teams that are loyal to their fearless leader (me) and to each other.

HERE ARE A FEW OF MY BEST TIPS FOR DOING JUST THAT:

1. **Communicate all the time,** and in plain language. When people feel included, people feel trusted.
2. **Teach your team.** When you spend time and energy on them, they feel valued.
3. **Ask for input from your team.** Your team will feel more invested in decisions.
4. **Expect big things.** When your team succeeds, they will feel important.
5. **Reward success.** People crave recognition and work harder when they get it.

What Have We Learned?

- *Loyal team members tell you the truth, even when it is hard to hear.*
- *To show your loyalty, don't criticize team members in public.*
- *Build loyal teams through communication, high expectations, and rewards.*

Acceptance

"I'VE BEEN HERE ALL YEAR"
by Pig-Pen

Thank you for reading my chapter. I apologize for the
smudges on some of the pages. As you probably know,
I'm a bit of a dirt magnet.

If it makes you feel any better, the cloud that surrounds me is the dust of ancient civilizations, so I have always considered it an honor to be in its midst.

Of course, not everyone shares my feelings—very few of the gang do. Only Charlie Brown has shown unconditional acceptance of my nontraditional lifestyle. That is one of the many reasons he is such a good leader of our baseball team.

He is my role model, and I think you can learn a lot from him. I know I have.

The Gift of Being Included

At some point in your life, you've probably known a great leader. What was it about them that inspired you? Energized you to do your very best?

I think back to the time when Charlie Brown directed the Christmas pageant. He could have listened to the rest of kids who didn't want me in the play. Instead, he cast me as the innkeeper, and convinced Frieda to play my wife.

It was an honor to be included in the production.

Charlie Brown's actions showed true leadership. Not only was he fair, but he also looked past the dirt and dust and saw my potential. His support made me want to give the play my very best, and I ended up working harder than I ever imagined.

Charlie Brown's behavior towards me is an example of inclusive leadership, which motivates people because they feel valued and respected, real members of a team working toward a common goal. And if everyone on the team is different from one another, that diversity is treated as an advantage, not a curse, because they each bring a unique point of view to the game or project.

I am trying to remember where I first learned about inclusive leadership...oh yeah! Sally did a report on it in civics class earlier this year.

Well, she got close anyway.

"A report by me, Sally."

ACCEPTANCE: ADDITIONAL POINTS FROM SALLY
This Is My Report on Reclusive Leadership.

It's important to know the difference between *reclusive* and *inclusive* leaders. Inclusive leaders are ideal and want to include coworkers in the process. Reclusive leaders grow beards and live in shacks. Inclusive leaders have two other qualities that also put them above reclusive ones—making their team members loyal and true!

They appreciate differences

Inclusive leaders like and encourage diversity in their teams, and are keenly aware of any stereotypes or disrespectful behavior. They are also open to learning new skills from the different people on their team.

For example, I often teach the gang new vocabulary words, since I know a lot of really big words, and then they help me understand the actual meaning and proper usage.

I believe that's what you call a win-win situation.

They encourage participation

An inclusive leader allows everyone to join in, speak up, and contribute. The team will have more confidence in the process if clear rules are created that cover questions and decision making.

For example, we could use rules for these reports... like, do I get extra credit? An ice cream cone? A kiss from my Sweet Babboo?

These things don't write themselves, people.

Marcie: Sir?

Peppermint Patty: What?

Huh...?! Marcie, I was asleep.

ACCEPTANCE: ADDITIONAL POINTS FROM MARCIE AND PEPPERMINT PATTY

Marcie: I'm sorry, sir. But I think any conversation about acceptance and diversity should include a discussion of the role of women.

Peppermint Patty: Of course...I'll get right on tha...zzzzzzz.

Marie: Sir, it's important! You're the manager of our baseball team, but other female role models are rare, even though studies have shown that companies with more women on their board of directors outperform those with fewer.

Peppermint Patty: Boards...women...zzzzzz.

Marcie: We have to figure out why women are still so underrepresented in leadership roles at the top. And since you are a leader, sir, you can make proactive changes to our organization so more women advance like you.

Peppermint Patty: Huh...what? Sure, I can! Um, what did you have in mind?

Marcie: Well, sir, since you asked:

- ✕ **Lead by Example.** If you show the team that you care about the role of women, they will.

- ✕ **Ask for Input.** Involve the team in any decisions or changes regarding diversity so they have more ownership, and then keep the lines of communication open.

- ✕ **Offer Training.** Even a short two-hour class can open eyes and create newfound respect for people different from ourselves.

- ✕ **Celebrate Differences.** Look for opportunities to not only recognize difference, but also accommodate any special needs when appropriate.

Uh...sir?

Peppermint Patty: I got all of that, Marcie. Now, here's a tip for you: silence is golden.

Marcie: Go back to sleep, sir.

Working with Different People

Did you notice how I included a lot of different people and their points of view in this chapter? I thought it was important, especially since we're talking about inclusion and acceptance.

But things can go awry pretty quickly with so many differing personalities, preferences, and points of view. Diversity is wonderful, but it still has to be managed!

That's why it's important to establish ground rules for your team. (Who knows more about the "ground" than me...am I right?)

Here are some steps that will keep your individual behavior focused on success, especially when the topic divides the team:

1. Have everyone individually list their top values.
2. As a group, agree on your top three to five values.
3. Discuss why each is important.
4. Decide how the team can strengthen core values and what behaviors should be avoided altogether.

Take our Christmas pageant. During rehearsals, our director Charlie Brown was very concerned that we follow a set schedule. But the gang really valued the fun aspect of putting on a play more—dancing, singing, etc. I'd like to think we ended up meeting somewhere in the middle, but it took an impromptu value discussion to make that happen.

What Have We Learned?

- *Inclusive leadership makes employees feel valued and respected.*
- *Inclusive leaders appreciate differences and encourage participation.*
- *Lead by example and establish ground rules for interaction.*

The greatest gift
that you can give to
others is the gift of
unconditional love
and acceptance.

Brian Tracy

9

Adaptability

"EVERYONE GETS AN EGG"
by Snoopy aka the Easter Beagle aka Joe Cool
aka World War I Flying Ace aka Joe Grunge

If you asked the rest of the gang about Joe Cool or
the Easter Beagle, they'd probably say, "Oh, those are
just imaginary characters that Snoopy likes to play

when he's bored or feeling silly or trying to pull one over on us."

But they'd be missing the point.

When the World War I Flying Ace appears on the scene, it's because he has talents that are perfect for problems that can be solved with flying. And the Easter Beagle only makes his eggy deliveries because the Easter Bunny can't always be at the right place at the right time.

My so-called "alter egos" are actually ways I have adapted my personality to better handle different situations. And we all know that being adaptable is an essential quality of any successful leader.

Are you as brave as the World War I Flying Ace? As generous as the Easter Beagle? As confident as Joe Cool? Here's how being adaptable can make you a better leader and team member.

- **Multiple Choices:** Adaptable people don't panic if their first idea is shot down. (Curse you, Red Baron!) They have second and third and fourth choices at hand, which ultimately makes them more creative and better team players.

- **Outward Calm:** When the unexpected occurs, adaptable leaders maintain their poise, and are able to make quick decisions based on new information. The team looks to them for confidence...just like everyone looks to the Easter Beagle for eggs.
- **Openness:** Leaders who are adaptable are willing to take on new roles, new projects, and new responsibilities. Change is a major stress producer—just ask Joe Grunge. If you can handle it and succeed, you will gain skills and move up in your organization.

"Be cool."

ADAPTABILITY: ADDITIONAL POINTS FROM JOE COOL

I can't believe they asked Snoopy to talk about adapting to change. I mean, he's my other half, but who's the better half?

Joe Cool, baby.

I invented adaptability. In fact, did I invent Snoopy? Hmm...there's a real chicken-and-egg conundrum. But take it from Joe Cool—if you want to be an adaptable leader, just do these five things every day:

1. **Forget the Rules.** Change something...a process, a routine. Perhaps stop doing it at all. For instance, if you're not cool? Stop that right now.

2. **Say No to "No."** When you feel pessimistic about a new idea, stop and ask questions instead. Think positive. Be cool.

3. **Embrace Change.** Are you facing a new technology, system, tool, or software? Be the first to use it, and then teach others. I teach people how to wear sunglasses morning and night—essential to true coolness.

4. **Adapt to Your Team.** Don't change who you are, just how you sometimes behave, so you can work

more effectively with teammates based on their skills and weaknesses.

5. **Consider the Time of Year.** Make the most from seasonal downtime. Change your focus and project schedule to get the most out of your team, your year, and your goals.

You got all that? Cool, cool.

"Curses, foiled again!"

ADAPTABILITY: ADDITIONAL POINTS FROM THE WORLD WAR I FLYING ACE

Here's the World War I Flying Ace, in the heat of battle, shots ringing out, the enemy drawing nearer.

My only chance at survival? Constantly changing my battle plan. Zigging when the Red Baron zags. Bobbing when he weaves.

Not changing the circumstances, but dealing with them better. Faster. Smarter.

So, if you're serious about your leadership skills and how they can not only help you but also your entire team, leave the puppies' advice for the Daisy Hill Puppy Farm and apply these battle-proven techniques.

1. **Adapt Constantly.** Does change come in a pattern? On a monthly schedule? I know the Red Baron never sends a schedule of when he plans to attack. So you must adapt on the fly too.
2. **Take Risks.** Sometimes you may need to take action with only partial information—half the battle plan, so to speak. If you are a perfectionist, remind yourself: good enough can sometimes be better than perfect.
3. **Know Yourself.** Let's face it—not everyone can be a

World War I Flying Ace. The emotions of change are more difficult than the logic behind it. When adapting is hard, work through it.

4. **Help Others.** Once you have your reactions under control, show empathy for your team members and help them adapt to the current atmosphere.

5. **Own the Change.** Being a leader means that any change on your team is "your" change, so you need to get behind it. If you don't believe in it, speak to your superiors and get the information that you need. If you still can't support the change, work to create a change you can support.

"When things feel out of control, don't focus on reducing what you don't know."

ADAPTABILITY: ADDITIONAL POINTS FROM JOE GRUNGE

Instead, focus on improving how you handle what you don't know.

Ambiguity isn't the problem.

(Just backing up what the Ace had to say.)

What Have We Learned?

- *Adaptable leaders maintain their poise and are open to new directions.*
- *Change something every day—a process, a routine—or stop doing something altogether.*
- *Don't concentrate on changing the circumstances; change your ability to handle them.*

Celebration

"HAPPINESS IS A BEANBAG CHAIR"
by Sally

Hi there!

Hope it's okay if I don't get up. There's nothing I like better in life than relaxing in my beanbag chair in front of the TV.

Did you know I went to beanbag camp once? It was the BEST. We learned how to sit in a beanbag chair and eat snacks at the same time. It takes some serious concentration.

(Not really.)

But I am exhausted from listening to the rest of the gang. **Work of any kind shouldn't be so much...well, work!** If you're going to get anything accomplished, you have to pace yourself, and plan time to take it easy. If you don't, you'll burn out, and even an afternoon of cartoons and cheese balls in a cushy beanbag won't save you.

So join me! Plop down in the nearest comfy chair—or at the very least, hug a warm puppy—and I'll show you how to turn those Type A tendencies of yours into a much more approachable C-minus.

And don't worry; I'll keep it simple. I only use controversial* English.

---

* Um, make that "conversational." Huh. That makes more sense too.

Hard Work Needs More Cushions

Any friend of mine knows I'm not a fan of hard work. School is the perfect example.

I HATE school! As soon as I learn one thing, the teachers go on to something else! When I first started, they taught me where the lunchroom was, and then expected me to remember how to find my desk.

It's like they want students to work hard in school, but don't care if the classroom or the lessons are helping us to make that happen. And we could all use a little help...am I right?

Fortunately, beanbag camp taught me nine methods on how to make work of any kind easier from the start!

1. Ask questions

At beanbag camp, my cabin chief loved pretzels. Served pretzels at every training session. The girls in my cabin? Not fans of pretzels. So our first classes were pretty disappointing. Lesson learned: Don't assume you know what the group needs or wants. Ask. You don't want to fail for the wrong reason.

2. Make adjustments

There's no "I" in "TEAM," but that's just a spelling thing. (I HATE spelling too.) Every team or office is made up of individuals who respond differently to rules, to each

other, and to the boss. So, if you're the boss, you need to manage each person in their own unique way. (Hear that, Teacher? I'm not my big brother, so stop treating me like him. I don't know my multiplication tables!!)

3. Know yourself

The gang has pointed out that I am quick to yell—and quite loudly—when I get frustrated. (I would like to disagree, but they have video.) All of us have a personal style that we need to be aware of, especially if we lead a group of people. This will be what they see and remember. And watch on video.

4. Snack breaks aren't just for kids

At beanbag camp, it was pretty easy to have fun. We were sitting on the world's most comfy chairs. We were given free snacks of our choosing (after the pretzel incident). And we got to watch television.

For the entire summer.

School will never be that fun. Although I have never had a real job, I've seen my dad cut hair at his barbershop, and even though they do have chairs, he admits that watching TV is better. Chances are, even on the best day, your job can't beat binge-watching Netflix and salty snacks.

That's why it's work.

But you can plan celebrations that make work less like work and more like beanbag camp. And by keeping these tips in mind, these moments will make work more fun for you and your coworkers.

5. Variety show

Spread out the celebrations throughout the year so folks have something to look forward to. Also, think about different sizes. For instance, at Halloween, only a couple of us celebrate the Great Pumpkin with my sweet Babboo Linus (for obvious reasons), but the whole gang takes part in the Christmas pageant.

6. The voice

Now, I'm not one to brag. (That would be Frieda, who can never stop talking about her naturally curly hair.) But think about giving your team a forum online or in a common area to share work achievements, client testimonials, and personal news. It will get the conversation started and help turn coworkers into friends!

7. Community calendar

The gang and I have trick-or-treated for charity ever since I can remember. Big brother always gets a rock, but it's a lot of fun and raises money for a good cause. Adding community events to your company's list is a great way to give back to your town while building team spirit.

8. Name that to-do list

Once you've come up with all the fun stuff—with suggestions from everyone on your team—it might be even more fun to name your program. Again, ask your team

for input, or make the naming process a competition with prizes.

9. Prizes like...a new car!

What? You don't give your team new automobiles as prizes? (They didn't at beanbag camp, either.)

Prizes are fun, no matter the size or cost, because people just love winning things. Need some ideas? I've got a few more affordable ideas:

- Free lunch
- Gift cards
- Office electronics (smartphone, tablet, laptop)
- Time off
- Paid vacation packages

If I could pick a prize, I would take my big brother's bedroom. I've wanted it for years. A couple of times, I almost got my stuff moved in, but then he came back. Those were dark days.

"Dear Sally..."

CELEBRATION: ADDITIONAL POINTS FROM CHARLIE BROWN

I agree; my bedroom is the perfect prize. But you will not get to live in it until I move out of the house.

So...probably never.

What Have We Learned?

- *Ask what the team wants.*
- *Plan celebrations throughout the year.*
- *Everyone loves free stuff.*

The celebration...
you cannot practice
it or anything. It's
a moment when the
excitement of your
goal makes you react
to the moment.

Peter Bondra

11

What Have We Learned, Charlie Brown?

CHAPTER 1: Perseverance

- ✘ Learn from failures.
- ✘ Get yourself a gang.
- ✘ Visualize the goal.
- ✘ Be positive.

CHAPTER 2: Presence

- ✘ The "It Factor" can be learned.
- ✘ Your physical habits define your presence.
- ✘ People remember how you make them feel too.

CHAPTER 3: Communication

- ✘ Write for your audience in a concise yet conversational style.
- ✘ Use formatting elements to make your document easy to skim.
- ✘ Allow ample time for proofreading—have a friend proofread if possible.

CHAPTER 4: Listening

- ✘ Evolution makes it difficult for us to listen.
- ✘ Pay attention when you listen (and show it).
- ✘ Use the LINUS mnemonic to become an active listener.

CHAPTER 5: Inspiration

- ✘ Great leaders find their passions and pursue them at any cost.
- ✘ Good leaders are always looking for new ideas and new information.
- ✘ You are the average of the five people you spend the most time with.

CHAPTER 6: Teamwork

- ✘ Know what kind of leader you are.
- ✘ Acknowledge your team's unique qualities and bring them together into a stronger unit.
- ✘ Use feedback to teach and praise.
- ✘ Make teamwork part of who you are: when your friend achieves, you achieve.

CHAPTER 7: Loyalty

- ✘ Loyal team members tell you the truth, even when it is hard to hear.
- ✘ To show your loyalty, don't criticize team members in public.
- ✘ Build loyal teams through communication, high expectations, and rewards.

CHAPTER 8: Acceptance

* Inclusive leadership makes employees feel valued and respected.
* Inclusive leaders appreciate differences and encourage participation.
* Lead by example and establish ground rules for interaction.

CHAPTER 9: Adaptability

* Adaptable leaders maintain their poise and are open to new directions.
* Change something every day—a process, a routine—or stop doing something altogether.
* Don't concentrate on changing the circumstances; change your ability to handle them.

CHAPTER 10: Celebration

* Ask what the team wants.
* Plan celebrations throughout the year.
* Everyone loves free stuff.

A good leader takes
a little more than his
share of the blame,
a little less than his
share of the credit.

Arnold H. Glasow

12

Pop Quiz

1. Charles Schulz modeled Snoopy after his childhood dog, a beagle named

   A. Spike.
   B. Olaf.
   C. Rover.
   D. Andy.

2. Charlie Brown decided to stay home with Snoopy instead of going to summer camp. This decision displayed his

   A. fear of insects.
   B. courage to be different.
   C. confusion with the summer vacation schedule.
   D. desire to be a dog walker.

3. When you look into your audience's eyes as you make a presentation, you appear everything BUT

A. confident.
B. prepared.
C. shifty.
D. expert.

4. Using formatting elements like bullet points,
   bold, and underline in your writing makes your
   document easier to

   A. skim.
   B. photocopy.
   C. scan.
   D. rephrase.

5. "Who," "What," and "When" are examples of what
   type of question that is useful in an interactive
   conversation?

   A. Open-ended
   B. Close-ended
   C. Greater response
   D. Redirection

6. Which of the following is NOT a quality of a leader who inspires his or her team to do great things?

   A. Interest in other people's lives
   B. Impressive vocabulary of swear words
   C. Sense of humor
   D. Being calm and reasonable in a crisis

7. Once you know your team members really well, make sure they each (1) know their role and (2) understand exactly what is expected of them in that role.

   A. True
   B. False

8. You can build a team that is loyal to their leader and to each other by

   A. encouraging infighting and competition.
   B. setting low expectations (so you're not disappointed).

C. communicating as much as possible.

D. rewarding employees only when your boss makes you.

9. When you start to feel pessimistic about a change in your life or work, what does Joe Cool recommend that you do instead?

A. Go on vacation immediately.

B. Ask questions to understand more fully.

C. Close your eyes tightly and scream.

D. Blame someone else.

10. Sally's suggestions for celebrations throughout the work year were inspired by her positive experiences with

A. beanbag camp.

B. detention.

C. birthday parties past.

D. parades.

ANSWER KEY

1. Charles Schulz modeled Snoopy after his childhood dog, a beagle named

    A. Spike.

2. Charlie Brown decided to stay home with Snoopy instead of going to summer camp. This decision displayed his

    B. courage to be different.

3. When you look into your audience's eyes as you make a presentation, you appear everything BUT

    C. shifty.

4. Using formatting elements like bullet points, bold, and underline in your writing makes your document easier to

    A. skim.

5. "Who," "What," and "When" are examples of what type of question that is useful in an interactive conversation?

   A. Open-ended

6. Which of the following is NOT a quality of a leader who inspires his or her team to do great things?

   B. Impressive vocabulary of swear words

7. Once you know your team members really well, make sure they each (1) know their role and (2) understand exactly what is expected of them in that role.

   A. True

8. You can build a team that is loyal to their leader and to each other by

   C. communicating as much as possible.

9. When you start to feel pessimistic about a change in your life or a work, what does Joe Cool recommend you to do instead?

   B. Ask questions to understand more fully.

10. Sally's suggestions for celebrations throughout the work year were inspired by her positive experiences with

    A. beanbag camp.

How did you do? Don't worry; we won't grade you. But if you got fewer than four correct, Snoopy is coming to your house and serenading you with howls.

Not ready for the concert? We didn't think so. Just take another shot at it, and when you get seven or more right, we'll tell Snoopy his novel has been published. (He'll come running.)

About Charles Schulz

It was a dark and stormy night—November 26, 1922, to be precise—when Charles Schulz was born in Minneapolis, Minnesota.

As a senior in high school, Schulz passed a talent test from Art Instruction Schools, took the course, and tried to sell cartoons for money.

It did not go well. At first.

Then, between 1948 and 1950, he sold seventeen cartoons to the *Saturday Evening Post*. For two years, he also drew a weekly comic called *Li'l Folks* for St. Paul *Pioneer Press*.

He submitted strips to the newspaper syndicates, and United Feature Syndicate was interested. But when Schulz met with the editors in New York City, they instead selected his sketches for a new comic strip that would be soon be called *Peanuts*.

The first *Peanuts* daily was published October 2, 1950; the first Sunday, January 6, 1952. And the last

Peanuts strip appeared February 13, 2000, the morning after Schulz passed away.

Schulz completed 17,897 daily and Sunday strips, writing, drawing, and lettering each and every one—an achievement unmatched in the industry.

Photo by Jean Schulz, courtesy of the Charles M. Schulz Museum and Research Center

About the Author

Carla Curtsinger is a writer, blogger, keynote speaker, and university lecturer. She fancies herself a bit of a Snoopy with a touch of Lucy's presence. Curtsinger got to know the *Peanuts* gang "up close and personal" when she was a writer and editor for Hallmark Cards in Kansas City, where she spearheaded *Peanuts* greeting cards for three years. She had the great honor of corresponding with Charles Schulz, who donated signed artwork for an auction to benefit a local animal shelter. Curtsinger holds a BS in communications from the University of Kentucky and a master's certificate in publishing from New York University. She lives in Manhattan.

NOTES

NOTES

_____

_____

_____

_____

_____

_____

_____

_____

_____

_____

NOTES

NOTES

NOTES